To WIT
and admiration.

# PARADISE TO PENTECOST
# AND BEYOND

In Christ,

# PARADISE TO PENTECOST AND BEYOND

Jane Cocke Perdue

authorHOUSE®

AuthorHouse™ LLC
1663 Liberty Drive
Bloomington, IN 47403
www.authorhouse.com
Phone: 1-800-839-8640

Published by AuthorHouse    01/25/2014

ISBN: 978-1-4918-5208-8 (sc)
ISBN: 978-1-4918-5207-1 (e)

Library of Congress Control Number: 2014900918

# Contents

OLD TESTAMENT

## THE NEW TESTAMENT:  THE BIRTH

## THE MINISTRY OF JESUS

# To Adam

As you strolled among blightless blooms
And heaven's hues spilling earthward,
As you tended Eden,
Was there bliss?
Or did the gnaw of loneliness
Eat away leaving you empty
Until another miracle of genesis,
The mate of God's creation,
Filled your hunger?
Explosion of ecstasy!
And in those moments,
A delusion of completeness
Became your nemesis—
Your failure to remember
It was God's intention
That you and she be garden tenders.

# Eve?

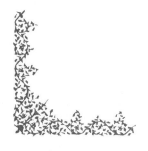

And Eve?
Did you feel fulfillment
and contentment
with God's first human
walking in the sunlight
sharing the wonder
or did you compete with Adam
to be first to find all knowledge
turning from your Creator?
Was there smugness on your face
as you pulled the fruit to taste
determining a destiny of doom
away from Paradise?

# Bone and Flesh

Flesh of my flesh,
Bone of my bone,
In this fresh luxuriant space,
This place of no shame,
You, my rib, my Adam,
Heard a warning,
A prohibition.

The condition of our bliss
Sounded in the morning.
A forbidden tree exists
Here where we till
And tend the ground.

Flesh of my flesh,
Hold my hand
So that God's command
Never to touch fruit forbidden
Will not be broken.

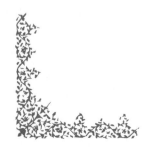

That hidden Serpent,
Coiled for invitation,
Hisses temptation—
His words spoken smooth
As pomegranate seeds
Would spoil our ecstasy,
Begging pride to reach
Toward near branches
Where temptation dangles
Ripening in sunlight.

Bone of my bone,
Hold my hand.
Keep it from grasping
The downfall
Of humankind.
Do not leave me alone
Here with God
In Paradise.

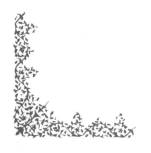

# Where Are You?

The fruit's delicious juices
Drool satisfaction from my lips
Followed by my first taste of shame
In the cool of Eden's garden.

The blame? Not my defying
But the lying snake lured us to disgrace
With open eyes our depravity assured
We know the destiny of pain.

Wrapped in quick-sewn leaves we kneel
In cover and feel God's footsteps
On the ground from which we came
God calling, calling through the trees.

"Come tell what you have done
In one act to please your appetites.
Where are you, Adam, my breath of life.?
And Eve, your helpmate, your wife?"

"Where are you? What have you done?
My garden tenders, my own images?
Where are you hiding? What have you done?"
Nighttime and darkness have come.

"Where are you? What have you done?"

# The Tempter

Your reputation made in The Beginning
wandering in a garden,
the story says,
on feet like ours
until your beguiling words
ended hours of bliss in Eden.
Eve heard your hissing first
as she stood weeping at the tree
bearing delicious fruit forbidden
while you, hidden in the shadows,
boldly stepped to her naked side.
Cunning, sly, coaxing her to disobey
that same day you became "The Tempter,"
first cause of Creation's fall,
cursed to the ground, destined to crawl
on your belly eating dust.
Humankind looks at you with fear
and horror at your death-inflicting power,
collectively remembering the day and hour
when your crafty words
caused an avalanche of disobedience
and aftermath of eternal pain.

# Garden of Return

God prepared such a garden—
Animals grazing in meadows
Of amazing abundance,
Birds resting on tree limbs
Forked for nesting,
Creatures wandering in ecstasy.

Then . . .
God's command to *tend*
The garden tested
Human desire to *own* the garden,
Causing the descent from grace.

Or was it ascent?

After the expulsion,
Appreciation for beginnings
Planted memory for beauty,
Stillness, peace, and love.

So we strive—
Reaching into fertile earth,
Planting seeds with hope
Each season of our lifetimes,
Knowing winter's gift of dying
Demands spring's birthing.

Eden will come again
When we truly tend the garden,
Careful not to scrape its surface,
Leaving barrenness
Or wound its innards
To please our passions
And fuel our pleasures.

Eden will come again
When Adam and Eve's progeny
Bless each other
In suffering and in celebration.
Eden will come again
When we hear God's voice
And are not ashamed.

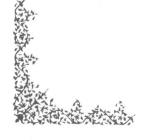

# Cain

The warmth of sunburst blossoms,
my heart's comfort.
Cooling springtime rains
create special offerings
to be gathered,
an appeasement to my God.
Abel's smelly goats
oozing sticky blood
dripping from the slaughter stone,
unacceptable gifts.
Special woven baskets
display my abundant sacrifice.
What will Abel use?
Whatever—
God will not affirm him!
And if God does accept his alms?
I will kill my brother Abel
and let his rich, red blood
nourish my lavish garden!
I am not obliged
for my brother's life!

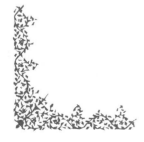

# Cain—After

Abel's screams in death endured,
his moans escaping from the ground,
uprooting my potential harvest
hurling me from my garden.
Wilderness-wanderer now I browse
where thorn and sting defend the living.
My protection, the mark of God—
an endless reminder.
I am obliged
for my brother's life.

# Noah

No safety or calm
Amid constant cacophony—
Screeching, screaming, scratching,
Stomping, bellowing, howling
Mass of fur and feathers,
Creatures rescued from oblivion
By my cunning and persistence
And God's insistence.

Water rising,
Wind threatening,
Boat rocking
For forty eternal days of chaos.

Finally beyond forever,
A strange stillness,
A bird returning with hope
Clamped in its beak,
An olive branch,
Salvation's symbol.
I was forever faithful
And God returned the favor.

# Fruit of the Vine

Denial—no! Not denial!
they knew; well they knew;
had watched his fall
from righteousness
and God's particular favor—
his fall so far—
this upright father
of their childhood
whose acts were legends
of faithful obedience.

Intoxicating juice
from Noah's vineyard
was the serpent
hissing in the jar
of fermentation,
winding around his life
of godliness, squeezing
until breath was gone
and his drunken stupors
became daily degradations.

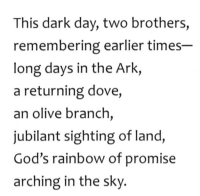

This dark day, two brothers,
remembering earlier times—
long days in the Ark,
a returning dove,
an olive branch,
jubilant sighting of land,
God's rainbow of promise
arching in the sky.

This day, two brothers
back into their father's tent
like children playing blind
drop a cloak
on his shriveled nakedness,
giving him a portion
of dignity long ago lost,
just as fig leaves sewn
covered Eve and Adam

Fruit again in the guise
of wisdom and contentment
caused another fall
and the shame of nakedness
became exponential
in humankind's wanderings
on God's good earth.

# The Scattering

The same dry dust
stirred by God's hand
to produce rusty Adam—
rained upon
wind-blown,
sun-dried
miracle of discovery
mixing elements
solid surprise of fired
building blocks—
square-stacked by desire
to reach the heavens.

In the scrambling upward
words were dropped
and lost,
ambition's weight
tumbled to the music
of Babel's confusing sounds
causing the fall—
clay crumbling to the ground.

In the Beginning,
the fall of creatures
reaching for forbidden fruit.

Next, Noah's descent
from righteousness
to drunken oblivion.

Now Babel's very people
bidding for the heavens,
strewn in separation
to the ends of earth.

Will the Word of Creation
redeem nations scattered
with one Almighty touch
of Rebirth?

# Word-filled

This day holds no promise
between yesterday and tomorrow.
Tired with worn out dreams
we bend to break until
this empty day is filled
with the Word
to wipe away all weariness.
Abraham and Sara
rubbed their eyes
in dusty disbelief
when strangers poured out
The Surprise!
So our impossibilities
fill with expectancy
brought by sojourners—
God's hovering Promise
To Be in the midst
of our wanderings.
The seed of Life!
And we laugh!

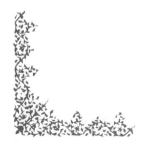

# Looking Back

Sand whipped and stung my eyes.
Silent pain does not compare
To burn of losing home and place.
I turned to stare through heat's fire waves
Wanting one last brief glance—
Sights familiar to retrieve
For losses I would always grieve.

Suddenly I froze in place
Not able to retrace my steps
Or move ahead to unknown space,
My eyes shed salt in streaming tears,
Freezing me into a pillar of fears,
Rooted by my past, now dead.
Ahead, the destination God had planned
As Lot's reward for faithfulness.

In one flash ray of desert sun
I have become a metaphor
Of dying grief, without a name—
"Lot's Wife" whose unforgiven sin
Was looking back towards her home,
Never to begin again.

# The Connector

Father Abraham with progeny equaling the stars
Cast aside Hagar's Ishmael to desert wandering
While his beloved only son by Sara,
Promised for eons,
Becomes of import only as a connector—
Deceitful son Jacob more memorable
Than laughing Father Isaac.

The link between tribal beginnings
And the nation Israel
May well have been sacrificed on Moriah,
Almost anonymous in Biblical lore.

Isaac, the connector,
In the chain of chosen ones
From Ur to Jerusalem,
Quietly walking the fields of his father,
Tending the herds, tenting,
Staying close to home,
Obedient to his father's selection,
Allowing himself comfort
With the chosen companion
As in the tent tears fell
On Rebecca's breast.

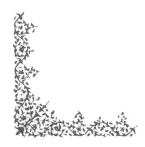

And when an old man, senile or sensible,
Choosing placation over peace
At the price of the elder twin,
Setting up a lasting feud
Of brotherly hate
With resolution yet to come.

And as all scoundrels, so like us
To give relief and satisfaction,
We choose one over the other,
Full-well knowing the difference
Between the hunter
And the one who tends the home fires.

# Brothers

The story is
Adam's loins
Eve's womb
gloom of sin
the beginning
the very
before twins
birthed in pain and blood
struggle to light waking
in stripped-naked infancy.

One mother's son
the other father's pride
two brothers
side by side.

Cain the garden tender
feels warm earth
remembers birth
plants seeds
watching with pride
blossoming abundance
in the sun.

Abel the herdsman
walks his flock
by still waters
stalks predators
lion-like
waits for the time
of weakness
inflicting death
by stone or spear
aimed to kill
spilling blood on sand
in land wild as
the taste of game.

Brothers
jealous rivals
raging fighting
staging struggles
for God's favor.
One day, Abel
reaching for a stone
sees behind
in dark a shadow—
brother Cain's
planter's rage
stages a murder
against innocence.

In the line of
Adam's progeny
twins entwined
hatefully before labor
begins and ends
with gasping grasping.
Jacob the deceiver
his mother's choice.
Esau another hairy hunter
walking in the desert
stalking prey into exhaustion
to please his father.

One doomed day
Jacob builds a fire
fills the pot
with lentils red
as Esau's beard.
He holds the bowl
of savory stew
taunting the hairy one
to trade his birthright
for a sated appetite.

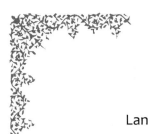

Landed inheritance
willed through deception
filled with generations
of warring tribes
marring land with battle sights
killing over water rights
and sacred stones
while Esau still grieves
his birthright
and his deceiving brother.

Cain alone
forever wanders
searching for a home.

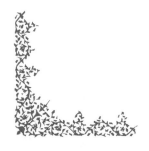

# Esau's Birthright

Exhaustion my nemesis—
Barren wasteland, cold, alone,
Frightened in darkness
As shadows move
To merge with terror.

Hunger becomes panic
In desert's emptiness.
Imagined scents
Of red meat juices
Drip from cacti thorns.

Smooth, rounded rocks
Become warm bread loaves.
I ache for home.
Driven by desire,
Far off I see smoke
Rising in promise
And vow to give all
For just a taste.

My supplanter waits
Cradling a steaming bowl
Of blood-red stew—
His victory assured.

# Leah, the Sister

The sight of Jacob caught my heart in hope,
Entering my father's home with swagger,
His eyes making inventory of our stores
And devouring my shapely sister Rachel.
He and father talked into the night
And struck a deal, a servitude of sorts,
Extended by custom and the trickery of a veil:
I would be the price for Jacob's Rachel.

The gift of many sons will turn his choice.
He must begin to look at me, the mother,
And know I am his open vessel
From whom has come his progeny.
But barren Rachel is still the one with favor,
His preference painful and transparent.
I am the bearer of his children;
She, the bearer of his heart.

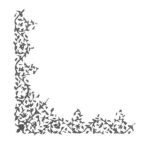

# Jacob's Journey

Nightmares invade sleep in homeward journeys.
Dreams resurrect separation's guilt,
Spilling remorse into wakefulness,
Sketching in the conscience clear regret.
Struggles end in maimed body parts.
Crippled by pressure of bargains struck with God
To satisfy the safety of our future,
In pain and dread, we face dawn's light
And cross Jabbok where our dearest possessions,
Unaware of survival's fight for blessedness,
Have been dispersed to wait our coming.

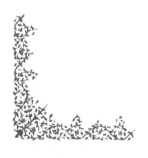

# Joseph, the Dreamer

My eyes burn to match the desert sun
As I seek my shepherd brothers— father's orders.
Such a long, lonely journey to their camp
To find them gone, searching for more pasture.

My knapsack heavy with food from home—
Figs and pomegranates to quench a thirst
And bread with honey for sustenance
To counter the bitter taste of cacti buds.

Months have passed since we were together
By the campfire outside our tent roasting young goats,
Battling with cooking sticks like fierce warriors,
Enmity present as our family circle loosened.

Father called me to him for special treats
And I saw their eyes blaze with jealousy,
Especially the day he gave me a ruler's coat
Finely made of multicolored cloths hanging royally.

Then, before this journey, my recurring dream.
I am to be a ruler— a nighttime prophecy.
Sheaves of wheat bow down to me.
Celestial bodies obey my commands.

Near Dothan, I see sheep in the distance,
My brothers scattered round like protective fences.
They issue no greeting as I approach, offer no water.
I have drunk the last of my supply hours ago.

Hands grab me roughly. I hear Reuben's protests
Before all is dark and dry in a deserted well.
What irony! I am thirsty! Oh, so thirsty!
Bone dry inside the well where I have been thrown!

Horse hoofs sound and the ground vibrates
Along with voices of negotiation, Judah's objections
And strange dialects sounding like impatient Ishmaelites.
I am pulled into the sunlight by strange hands.

Not the first to be betrayed for the price of silver.
Certainly not the last! I am a victim of jealousy like Abel,
Esau's descendant banished to a foreign land.
Riding away from home, I am weak with fright.

My ruler's cloak has been stripped away, evidence of my "death."
I am the prelude to another story of prophetic truth.
Jealously, betrayal and descending into thirsty darkness.
In God's time I become the ruler of my dreams.

I am the savior of my brothers who betrayed me.
They do not know me, but they have come in desperation
To the place where I offer them forgiveness
And the bread of life to save them from their deprivation.

# Moses

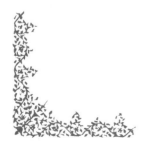

Muddy river waters carried me to a palace
Wrapped with royal gardens filled with loveliness.
Mere glances yielded my desires.
But watching servants bent and humble
I wished to take their burdens as my own.

In manhood, the certitude of my station
Of sojourner in Pharaoh's world solidified.
One day erupting in the marketplace of my people
I killed a citizen of Pharaoh's province
As he struck my undefended countryman

Internal struggles between royalty and servanthood
Ended in my murderous act. I became an instant fugitive,
Looking over my shoulders for years and years,
Until one day a desert bush gave me my destiny,
Enflaming me with passion for the freedom of the Hebrews.

# Bull Rush Baby

Bull rush baby,
river swept to Pharaoh's palace,
suckled by your secret mother,
your true identity erupting
with a murder in the marketplace.

Instant Hebrew fugitive
glancing ever backward,
Midian gave you a well of hope
as Jethro's shepherd
until a desert bush inflamed you
with Yahweh's mandate
to lead the march to freedom,
under the banner of God's Promise.

# Blood Offering

Bloating, screaming, moaning,
spurting blood from slain lambs
while Yahweh's messengers,
gripping swords of death,
turn aside from lintels
marked by hyssop's blood-brush.

Chosen Ones with ready staffs
march through parted waters
to years of lonely wandering—
freedom's price for uncertainty.

Would they rather stay behind
in slavery's shackles,
their stomachs filled
with fish and leavened bread,
their spirits emptied,
building foreign empires,
while leeks and garlic
offer flavors not found in manna?

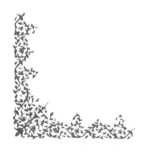

# A Mother's Coat

I tenderly stroke the linen
remembering Samuel must be cold
in the drafty temple
    and lonely
       in the night
with only Eli's wheezy snoring
sounding so far from home.

Our pilgrimage begins in just two days.
Elkanah gathers offerings
For Shiloh's altar.

I feel the coat again
and kneel in thankful prayer
knowing I will be empty-handed
    going
my sacrifice already there
waiting for the coat
I, his mother, make each year
taking warmth and wrapping him
in dedication—

My provision for my son
God's chosen one.

# God's Tough Love

Eli's eyes failed to see
his scoundrel sons
The parental flaw, denial,
scrawled hope
on his father's heart
awed by love.

God's words
echo in the temple
as Eli listens
from his dying bed-
no priestly dynasty
as God once said,
instead Hannah's son
The Chosen One.

Samuel so small
runs frightened
in the shadows
"Did you call?"
Groaning with despair
Eli barely sees the child
he wishes were his own.

# David's Penitence

War-weary, I chose a respite,
my kingly option.
Leadership required renewal,
solitary evening silence
to ponder destruction
and prevent defeat.
The army's absence,
a shadowed vacancy
in my city home-of-the-ark.
Jerusalem rested to receive
the dark of evening.
Imperceptible movement
snagged my vision
in the dusky distance—
a woman bathing,
sensuality in twilight.
Reflection imploded
into lust,
snatched reason
and faithfulness,
guaranteed destruction
and defeat.

# David's Dairy

Dark dreaded predators
soundlessly prowling the perimeter
listening for helpless bleats
signaled from their victims.
Saul's incessant jealousy,
deception and depression.
Countless outlaw battles
and conniving covenants.
Sorrow diminished victory;
sin defeated faithfulness.
Nathan, my ceaseless conscience.
Bathsheeba's first-born dead.
Absalom's rebellion and hanging death.
My heartfelt sorrow,
bending into dying years,
the knowledge of my sins.

Goliath was the easiest.

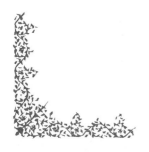

# Why?

Job's question reappears in daily form;
Small deaths cause reawakened grief;
We question in the dark all suffering;
Black, unjust rages bring short-term relief.
Our well-intentioned comforters appear
On the fringes of desperation.
We tout innocence to those who listen
Resisting the injustice of our plight.

Are we now punished for sinlessness?
Given pain as reward for constant faith?
Is God the heavenly puppeteer?
Guiding feet through impassable paths
Until we cannot run or walk or stand?
We mourn the deaths of those who loved us.
Should we allow ourselves to curse and die
Thinking God is absent from our agony?

Tribulation seems to know no end.
There is nowhere consolation.
Birth, the world, our plight have no meaning.
Is this God's vendetta for Creation?
Is there reason for unending suffering?
No answer here, only God is with us—
Emmanuel, our Suffering Servant.

# From the Heart

Before our infant cries
of desperate discontent,
our hearts beat within the womb.
In pre-birth innocence we grew.
Oh Lord, our God, you knew
our hearts and bodies, souls and spirits
knit together by your creative love—
your beloved ones
nourished by life's blood pumping
through our bodies
rocking in fluid safety.

Renew those pure hearts now
with innocence apart
from worldly knowledge
and discontent—
a cleansing so your gift of love
will flow to give new life
in dreaded places,
lifting us who fall
heavy with hopelessness,
dreads and doubts.

Again, oh God, renew our hearts!
Let them beat with the rhythm
of your unending love,
giving us Eternal Life!

# In Ordinary Time

Womb-fresh Baby God
In and hollowed-out manger,
Holding fresh hay for you—
A place to lay your head
Where warmth and sustenance
Are offered to your creatures
In ordinary time.
On Christmas Day,
This is your birthing place.

Wound-fresh Man God
On a hate-hewn cross,
Molding awful death for you—
No place to lay your head.
Agony and love
Offered to the world
In ordinary time.
Our gift of Christmas,
This is your dying place.

World-fresh Spirit God,
In our desperation days,
Folding miracles in our midst—
A place to lay our heads.
Your gift of Life
Offered to the world
In ordinary time,
New births of joy and love,
This is your living place.

# In Utero

Mary, Immaculate, meek, mild
miraculously impregnated
still a child
finds Hannah's heart rhythm
heroine of ancient lore
barren woman
empty no more,
proclaiming God's goodness
filling her void
vowing a world upside down
power to the powerless.
In Mary's womb
throbs another heart
promising eternal life
to those without hope.
Does that tiny embryo
rocking in nascent bliss
hear his mother's Magnificat
and in his later years
remember the proclamation
"God will satisfy the hungry"
commanding his followers
to do the same?

# God's Love Cry

Swaddled in love
God squalls in a stable.
A child-baby
Becomes an offering to the world.
Our hope is helpless.
God's Love is crying
In the Christmas night.

Has it been forever?
A newborn's cry
Reclaims Creation!
We reach to touch
Heaven's hand of infancy,
Glimpsing a star's reflection
In eyes that look beyond forms
Into the human heart.

# The Eternal Story

The story pours from The Beginning
seeping into our Decembers—
endless telling, wonder humming,
celestial choirs sounding alleluias,
a father, mother and new-born baby,
angels, shepherds, an inn, a manger.
Later, star-gazing travelers,
an angry king
until . . .

A young man travels
in a caravan of pilgrims
to a Holy Place
and stays behind
to listen and to learn.

Jesus, the Child, becomes a Man
in the Temple of His faith.
God's will revealed
by questions posed and answered,
minds blended in wonderment
at this young man
who will later turn the tables
in the courtyard of this sacred space,
demanding reformation,
promising Life Eternal
here and now.

After three long years of crowds,
miracles and adoration,
the tables turn again
as a lonely, frightened few
watch on The Hill
when blood and sweat
pour together from the Cross
and Jesus asks His final question:
"Why?"

At Christmastime the answer—
God's Spirit pours
from the Beginning
into the midst of a stable.
God—
Was, Is, and Shall Be—
Then, Now and Always.

# So Far

So far from Eden's lush abundance
God's tenderness for Creation
cries in a stable.

So far from Messianic hopes
crafted through the years
God's love lies in a manger.

No jealous tyrant rules God's Kingdom
but a baby swaddled in helplessness
attended by creatures Adam named
in the beginning.

God's amazing conception
birthed outside the box—
So far from human expectation.

# Battlefield Christmas

Baby born of God's love,
This is your humble home place,
This space of strife and war
So far from your intentions.

Boy soldiers, guns hoisted,
Keep watch in silence
As night's black drop-cloth
Drapes over desert hills.

Refugees crowd dusty roads
Holding haunted children
Who scream in the hush
Spliced between bombings.

Evening stars break the gloom
With heavenly lights of wonder
And soldiers become shepherds
In these fields of battle—

Listening to angels singing,
Bringing hope in tones
Of splendor begun in Eden
And climaxed in a manger bed.

# Midwife

If Jesus were born today
Would his cry echo where he lay
Between tenements and store fronts
In places where children play
Games of temptation defying death
As if there were no desperation?

Would Joseph and Mary join
A worming caravan of refugees
Leaving home in quiet panic
No ease in trudging ancient paths
With family and strangers
To no certain destination?

Could the Star of Bethlehem shine
Dangling rays of hope from the sky
Through destitution's darkness?
And angels' messages be heard
Above gunshots in the streets
Confounding night's stillness?

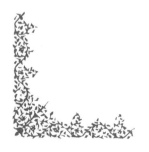

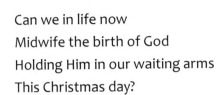

Can we in life now
Midwife the birth of God
Holding Him in our waiting arms
This Christmas day?

God's Holy Child born
God's Love manifest
Who has no place to rest his head
But in our hands and hearts.

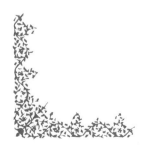

# Cranberries

Womb-fruit metaphor,
Globe-shaped perfection,
Bittersweet condiment,
Cranberry rich reminder,
Sour taste of hyssop
And sweetness of completed love.

Wound-fresh Messiah,
Red sustaining fruit
Spilling blood of suffering
For all the world.
Oh, Christ!
Your splitting, tearing crucifixion
Becomes our completion.

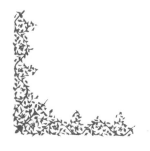

# Unexpected

Eve's fresh-formed hand
reaches away from God's command
rejecting Eden's lush perfection.

Abraham listens and obeys
moving family from homeland
tenting his way into Canaan.

Baby Moses destined to be slain
floats in a basket sealed
to mighty Pharaoh's daughter.

David youngest son of Jesse
chosen from a shepherd's field
anointed by Samuel's horn of oil.

Elizabeth's barrenness denied
by God's holy intervention
giving birth to John the Nazarene.

Mary lowly handmaid startled
by the Spirit's intervention
exulting in God her Saviour.

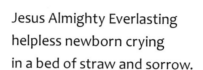

Jesus Almighty Everlasting
helpless newborn crying
in a bed of straw and sorrow.

God Incarnate; divine descension
all our notions defying—
a Messiah in a manger.

# Cathedral at Christmastide

*Attention must be paid!*
Meandering tourists,
mesmerized by opulence,
oblivious of sanctity,
shuffle past shrines
checking off attractions
on crumpled "must-see" lists.

*Attention must be paid!*
Knees flex against velvet,
hands press in expectation,
petitioners' humming drone
fills the hive of holiness
where gathered faithful
inhale a precious fragrance.

*Attention must be paid!*
Coins minted in hope
tremble through slits
in scarred collection boxes
smoke-dusted by flames
waving desperate prayers to Jude,
patron saint of hopeless causes.

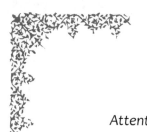

*Attention must be paid!*
Supplicants veiled in black,
wide-eyed communicants,
devout doubters
whose saints have died
to rise yet again
in dark suffering and failure.

This Season's humble hope—
God's Love in unblemished flesh
answers anguished prayers
with His palpable presence,
invading life and death,
binding wounds of loneliness.

*Attention has been paid!*

# Battlefields Undefined

All on earth watch the sky and pray
for the day of peace to come.
Do heralds of heaven sing within these bounds
above sounds of airborne weaponry?
Do visitors from far kingdoms still pay homage
and the downtrodden on hillsides kneel in hopefulness
before innocence birthed by God's tender mercy?

Some with sacrificial zeal
strap real bombs around their waistbands,
dying with their appointed victims
on battlefields undefined by armies.

To this place, this living space,
a conqueror in infant form
brings the ploughshare of peace
and straps to his pierced and bleeding body
the eternal explosive of salvation.

The sky erupts with God's Almighty Word
heard in celebration of all creation's hope
crying in a manger.

# God's Supplication

Strange—this misplaced manger
resting beside skyscrapers
beehives filled with workers
buzzing for survival

Strange—this cattle trough
sounding a newborn's cry
heard on lonesome highways
ribbon-like beside refineries
working overtime
fueling our human races.

Strange—this hay-filled box
contradicting our chaos
startling us to hear
instant messaging from angels.

Strange—this barn bassinet
holding helplessness
infant arms reaching out
God's supplication
inviting us to love.

The Beginning, Alpha,
filling our days
with grace amazing
facing whatever comes
before Omega.

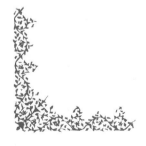

# Joy

Joy . . .
color waving
restless breezes brushing
the periphery of pleasure
inviting dances of celebration—
spectators or not.

Joy . . .
deep, throbbing beats
vibrations within the heart
pumping energy and expectancy
into each life's act—
even in silence.

Joy . . .
movement shaking
from the very bones
of newborn and dying
who recognize a reason
to disturb the stillness.

Joy . . .
infusing disappointments
with hopeful dreams
sending party invitations
for no commemoration
except being alive.

# Some Heard Angels

Stars shone in the Israeli sky.
Some heard angels singing.
I, clinging to duty,
Preferred lonely isolation.

Excited shepherds left hillsides
Expecting surprise like children.
Watching them disappear into Bethlehem,
I wished for such abandon.

Later they told stories of that night
When star's light shone
Upon a baby lying in a trough —
Humble creatures nudged by holiness.

Night-tenders and wisdom-seekers there
Knelt in prayer and heard angelic echoes
Proclaiming this newbon The Word,
God's rebel sigh.

And I?

# New Birth

The softest whimper
Rouses us from deep sleep
To serve our baby's need
To feed and clean and comfort
In the troubled night.

We lay aside all duties
But tending the arrival,
Sending us into servitude
For this tiny baby,
Nude, squalling, calling.

Noises of helplessness,
Cries never stilled,
We stand filled with awe
At raw creation's sound
In dawn's light.

Oh, Jesus! You also came,
God's helpless Infant Son.

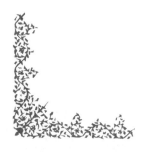

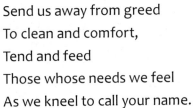

Send us away from greed
To clean and comfort,
Tend and feed
Those whose needs we feel
As we kneel to call your name.

In the stillness
Of this Christmas,
Help us to know
You have claimed the hearts
Of us on earth
By your very birth.

# Seamless

In the beginning
The Word
God wrapped in swaddling cloths
Skies bursting with song
Hope reborn
Nursed by expectation
Beyond comprehension
Crying in a manger
Far from home.

In the end
God's flesh
Stripped and whipped
Soldiers gambling beneath a cross
Tossing dice
For his seamless garment
On the hillside of his agony
Jesus cries for Abba
Far from home.

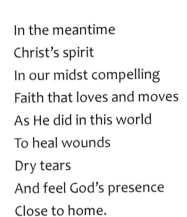

In the meantime
Christ's spirit
In our midst compelling
Faith that loves and moves
As He did in this world
To heal wounds
Dry tears
And feel God's presence
Close to home.

# Temple of Flesh

She was chosen, my betrothed—
promised to me by family tradition
and expectation to bear my progeny.

We were unknown to one another,
barely had we spoken,
yet I watched her belly swell
and wondered how
she lost her innocence?
to whom? and when?

She would be stoned for such,
so I offered privacy
to save her from disgrace—
a plan thwarted in the night, a voice:

"Take her Joseph; she is innocent.
God builds in such a way
you cannot comprehend.
Do not send her away.
She bears God's Temple of the Flesh."

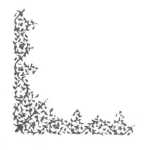

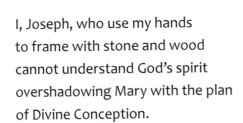

I, Joseph, who use my hands
to frame with stone and wood
cannot understand God's spirit
overshadowing Mary with the plan
of Divine Conception.

How near death came to her
before His birth,
had not an angel's tongue
proclaimed her innocence!

How soon death would come
by human misconception
to God's Masterpiece!

Finally, another intervention—
God's Temple resurrected,
offering hope to those
stoned in innocence,
love to those captive to injustice,
faith to those whose doubts paralyze,
forgiveness to the unforgiven
and Life Eternal to humankind!

# What If?

What if
Rome had not marched
Heavy-stepping through Palestine
Demanding tax enrollment
From citizenry under hardship?

What if
Joseph were self-righteousness
Convinced his betrothed
Deserved at least a stoning
In the public square
For her shameful pregnancy?

What if
Mary lacked naiveté
Refusing to hear voices
Beyond her understanding
Or kneeling in submission
To receive God's overshadowing
Gift to the world?

What if
The inn in Bethlehem
Had room to spare
And on that cloudy night
No stars were seen nor angels heard
Hovering above the manger
Like a heavenly afterbirth?

What if
Shepherds on the hillsides
Never looked beyond
Their nighttime campfires
To be energized by hope
And God never came to us
In swaddled love?

What if
God's earthbound revelation
Had not stretched his hands
From crib to cross
Lifting the humble
Feeding and comforting
Touching and healing
Walking paths of love and peace?

Then you and I would
Be in dark valleys
Stoning the innocent
Tending our investments
And dying our deaths—

Instead . . .

# Birth-bursting

Childhood left the day
Waking with dread and wonder—
What to do?
Should I do?
What if I don't?
Horizons gray and dark,
Frozen-still and cold.

Call back the child
Expecting many births,
What next again so wonder-filled?
    It will be!
        And if not,
    It will be again!
        Warm-blooded . . .
        Life-flowing . . .
        Red-bursting . . .
        Sun-rising . . .
A new day breathing!
A child returning!

# Judgment

"He will not amount to anything."
A slow, indulgent smile spreading boldly,
A dismissing hand waving
The finality of an edict.
Amount to whom?
The public or the private?
Himself?
Or others who measure lives
In opinions?
Does verbal issue create truth
To those who listen in agreement?
Perhaps . . .
See his face
Mirroring gentleness
and self-containment,
A certain mystery,
An untapped source of contentment,
Waiting for whatever experience.
He will be who He is
And his amount is not of import.
His life, however, is.

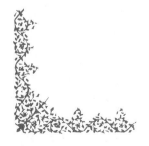

# Another Story

Another story line
for that famous prodigal . . .

The younger son does not return
with pig-sty mud clinging to his feet
and marks of squalor stamped
on his face and robe
badges of worthlessness
when he shuffles up the dusty road
his father running to meet him
without dignity.

The father's vigil is endless
as wind-blown dust creates false hopes
and movement of distant animals
mimic human shadows in the sun.

The prodigal never comes
falling for forgiveness
begging for servanthood
dreading his sullen brother
as the music and dancing begin.

The father through the years
remembers—
the birth
the child
the youth—
watching emptiness . . .

# To Be Continued . . .

So . . . he has returned and turned
this household upside down
I the elder brother driven out
like Ishmael and Esau.
My family's rightful heir
duty-bound these many years
of his cavorting recklessness—
now cast into a wilderness of rage
at the sight of father's ring
flashing from the hand
of my younger brother.

Vibrations of music
smell of roasting meat
dancing celebrations
of the rogue's arrival—
the one who squandered
wandering in debauchery
receiving all honor
and blessing
eating like a king
laughing without remorse
for wasted years.

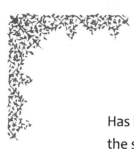

Has he forgotten
the scene of his departure
his mean demands, threats,
the storm of his leaving
and the sorrow of our father?
His return now desperation
to avoid starvation.
When the party ends
and his belly is full
will he stay
or is this return
his grand manipulation?

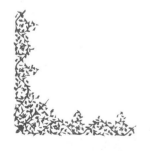

# Envisioned

Darkness wraps me— a cloak that does not warm.
I tear its edges loose to search for light.
Whose awful sin gave me these sightless eyes?
Whose trespasses left me here in night?

What transgressions fell on innocence,
Bequeathing me these days of desperation?
I, deprived of dignity, stripped of pride,
Begging, offer God sincere oblation.

Cold, wet mud rubbed gently on my eyes—
"This blind man is no sinner, nor his kin.
Go wash in waters God provides.
Your sight is restored; you are whole within."

I hurry to the pool of Siloam.
I am clean. He has restored my vision.
The crowd does not believe the miracle.
His loving act has only caused division.

The Pharisees are full of accusations
Regarding rules of Sabbath being broken.
The crowd unsure of my identity.
I? I only know my Lord has spoken.

# One Question

What must I do?
What else?
The question
like wind-whipped desert sand
stings my conscience.
What must I do?
What deed is needed?

Does He not know
my just rulings
faithful and obedient
to Moses' law?

From childhood
I have grown in wisdom
and stature
as did Samuel
in ancient times.
Now I am mature
but young, a ruler . . .

God rewards the righteous
with abundant possessions.
My cup overflows.

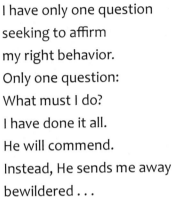

I have only one question
seeking to affirm
my right behavior.
Only one question:
What must I do?
I have done it all.
He will commend.
Instead, He sends me away
bewildered . . .

Did He say *"All my goods?"*

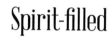

# Spirit-filled

Denying myself? How possible?
Draining my essence? How dangerous!
Risking my own death? How daunting!

Asking my memory to deny
days and years spent
acquiring congratulations?

Forgetting myself for others?
Making room to serve and love and tend
without attention or adulation?

Only by responding to One
who promises a Spirit
filling those risking loss
with gain in a kingdom misunderstood.
for the sake of One
who makes room for us
in His own emptiness.

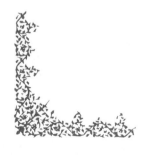

# The Gerasene

At first a brand new life ahead,
healed in a moment from the dead,
chains falling from my hands and feet
freeing me to clasp my savior.

My desire was to follow Him
wherever he worked miracles,
my testimony in my bearing—
proof that sanity could be restored.

But He told me to go home
and tell news of thwarted demons
to those who knew me best,
who remembered years of my insanity.

Often I wonder how it would have been
had I not stayed in this familiar place
where legions that possessed me
live every day in suspicious glances.

No one has forgotten the script written
in which I starred as a mad man.

# Who Not?

We reclined
with wine and bread
that dreaded last time together,
some still wanting
Roman restitution
throughout the land
led by our band
of faithful followers.
Others argued
claiming favor
in the kingdom coming.

He was silent,
then He turned
and softly spoke
words that echo
even now:

*One of you . . .*

How?
When?
Why?

Would we betray
this wise and gentle One?
At that moment
we all knew like David
when Nathan spew
the words:
*Thou art the man!*
In the shame
of the next few hours,
we each
would have Judas' name.

# Economics

What is the gain?
Wall Street or my soul?
Where is heaven's profit?
Adam Smith's "invisible hand"
writes history's tomes
while God's omnipotent hand,
pierced by greed's nail,
bleeds for us
who read market reports
clutching our thirty pieces of silver.

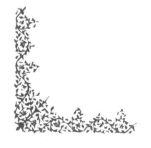

# A Tree to Climb

Come down, Zacchaeus!
Come down from your tree!
Right now I am coming to your home
To dine, break bread, drink wine
And talk of rejection, yours and mine—
Of being misunderstood, maligned.
You will not have to climb again to see.
That tree is mine . . .
On Calvary.

# Palm Sunday Eve

Tomorrow begins the ending.
Tomorrow ends the beginning.
A parade—
triumphal or pitiful—
trumped up by stage hands
manipulating majesty
without understanding
God Almighty's death wish,
apex of incarnation,
no helpless suffering,
but agony of One Chosen
demonstrating Love intended,
misunderstood by most
who cry Hosanna
(death is not blessed
unless defied
by a majestic Messiah)
while Nazareth's wanderer
walks straight into Gethsemane
and weeps
for all of us.

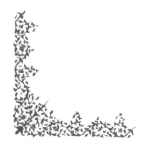

# Vultures Roosted

Clacking in ceremony,
vultures gather at the edges
tearing His words apart—
tongues sharpened
by the two-sided file
of consensus and opinion:

"No credentials, this son of Joseph,
His stories confounding,
His followers undesirable,
His message lacking
The Baptist's fire,
such arrogant claims,
His crowd diminishing,
His treasury low;
He will not last many days . . ."

And Jesus continues walking
to Jerusalem,
to Gethsemane,
to Golgotha.

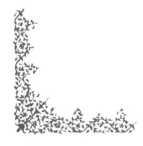

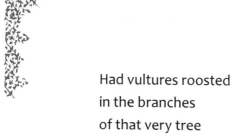

Had vultures roosted
in the branches
of that very tree
chopped down to make a cross
for such a routine,
hillside crucifixion?

The Word rejected
as God turns the world
upside down
in Resurrection.

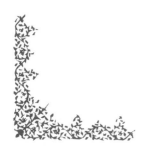

# The Women

Cast in The Word as tempters—
In the Beginning
Plucking Eden's fruit forbidden,
Later . . .
Seductive beauties
Tempting foreign royalty
Or dancing at a birthday feast
Demanding John The Baptist's
Severed head resting on a dish—
Women manipulating destiny.

Brave women, too, had roles to play—
Sarah joining Abraham
In endless wandering
Towards the Promised Land.

Miriam, her brother's savior,
Dancing to the sound of tambourines,
Writing triumphal songs of praise
Giving God the glory
For Israel's freedom march.

Rahab's risky rescue
For God's Chosen;
Micah's saving-life faithfulness
To her husband David,
Thwarting Saul's intent to murder.

Finally . . .
Ignoring danger of recognition,
Women on Golgotha's lonely hill—
Women who had trudged dusty trails
With The Rabbi and His Twelve,
Watching slow and painful death
With wrenching sadness.

Women—
First to proclaim
A Risen Lord
Of Resurrection!

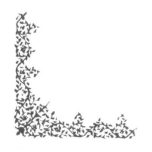

# Luck of the Draw

Judas was dead,
hanging in disgrace
to be replaced
in the group of twelve.

The plan? To draw lots
between Matthias and me.
I, Barsabbas, wanted in.
Had I not been
with each of them
in villages and fields
when Jesus taught
and healed
and gathered crowds?

Had I not paid my dues
by leaving friends
and family,
going where He went,
sometimes hungry,
always thirsty, spent?

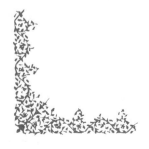

I watched their vying
for position
in His mission
even as He told
of His own dying.

Fair or not,
lots drawn decided.
my life's direction.
Just as I feared—
with one selection
my future disappeared.

Matthias won the draw.

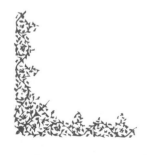

# Wilderness Mirage

Water flows abundantly across desert arroyos
While sapping sun draws out each drop of body fluid
And death's threat blinks in every glistening grain of sand
Proliferating such wasteland. Mirages signal hope.

Is this appearance or apparition born of desperation?
My body drained dreamless creates its own images
Of rebirth and resurrections tempting on the horizon,
Hurling me forward with the knowledge of my dying.

The familiar form does not dissipate as I approach.
Healing hands unlock revealing nail prints
As real as my own desperate longing to believe
His death was temporal— His life immortal.

# The Banquet

No silver goblets, white linens,
wine, reclining guests
or servants offering trays
heavy with abundance.
No candelabras shining,
cradling soft flames,
or imported dancers
swaying between banquet tables.
No native tricksters
with confounding magic,
but a seaside fire
burned to embers,
waiting to welcome workers
with gifts of food and warmth
at a long day's end,
or a lonely place crowded
with guests invited,
bringing baskets of fish and bread—
friends and neighbors
daring to divide their meal
with strangers.

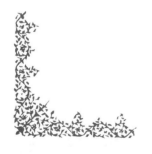

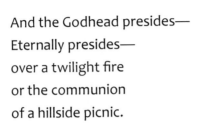

And the Godhead presides—
Eternally presides—
over a twilight fire
or the communion
of a hillside picnic.

Yes, that is the Kingdom!
The Kingdom come
on earth as it is in Heaven!
God's Everlasting Banquet!

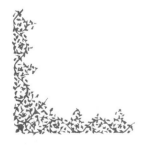

# Pentecost

Wind's swift burst,
fire flames lapping heat
lifted us from dejection.
Powerful spirit penetration
brought resurrection, renewal.
God's breath poured, filled,
gifting second life
from our birthing cries.

Hope-crazed, we spoke
to street strangers
clacking sounds from other lands,
meeting stares and glares
from doubters of our celebration.

Together in place as one
transformed body of believers.
Had we not gathered there,
we would grow old
without our dreams,
be young with no grand visions,
living as before—
captives of dread and fear
each one

alone . . .

by Jane Cocke Perdue

# They Told Me

They told me He would someday come
and wipe away all tears.
They told me,
those earnest teachers
wearing glasses on neck chains,
ruffled blouses and square-toed pumps,
classic suits with antique brooches.

They told me He would come
and wipe away all tears.
They told me,
but I barely cared,
sitting cross-legged
on the church basement floor
with my best friends,
giggling through the hour.
I had no tears.

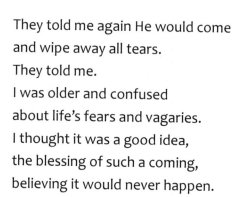

They told me again He would come
and wipe away all tears.
They told me.
I was older and confused
about life's fears and vagaries.
I thought it was a good idea,
the blessing of such a coming,
believing it would never happen.

They told me other things,
those blessed teachers.
They said Baby Jesus cried
His first earthly sound
in a manger long ago
and again as a grown man,
He cried for a friend
and later for Jerusalem.
At the end
He cried in a garden
and finally from the Cross—
Such a comfort when my tears
would not stop flowing.

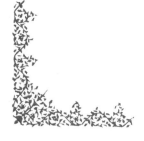

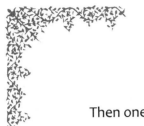

Then one day He came
as I was told He would,
but they were wrong,
those teachers so good.
He did not come
to wipe away all tears.
*He came and cried with me!*

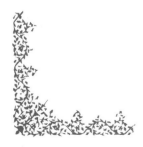

Made in the USA
San Bernardino, CA
14 September 2016